AF429000

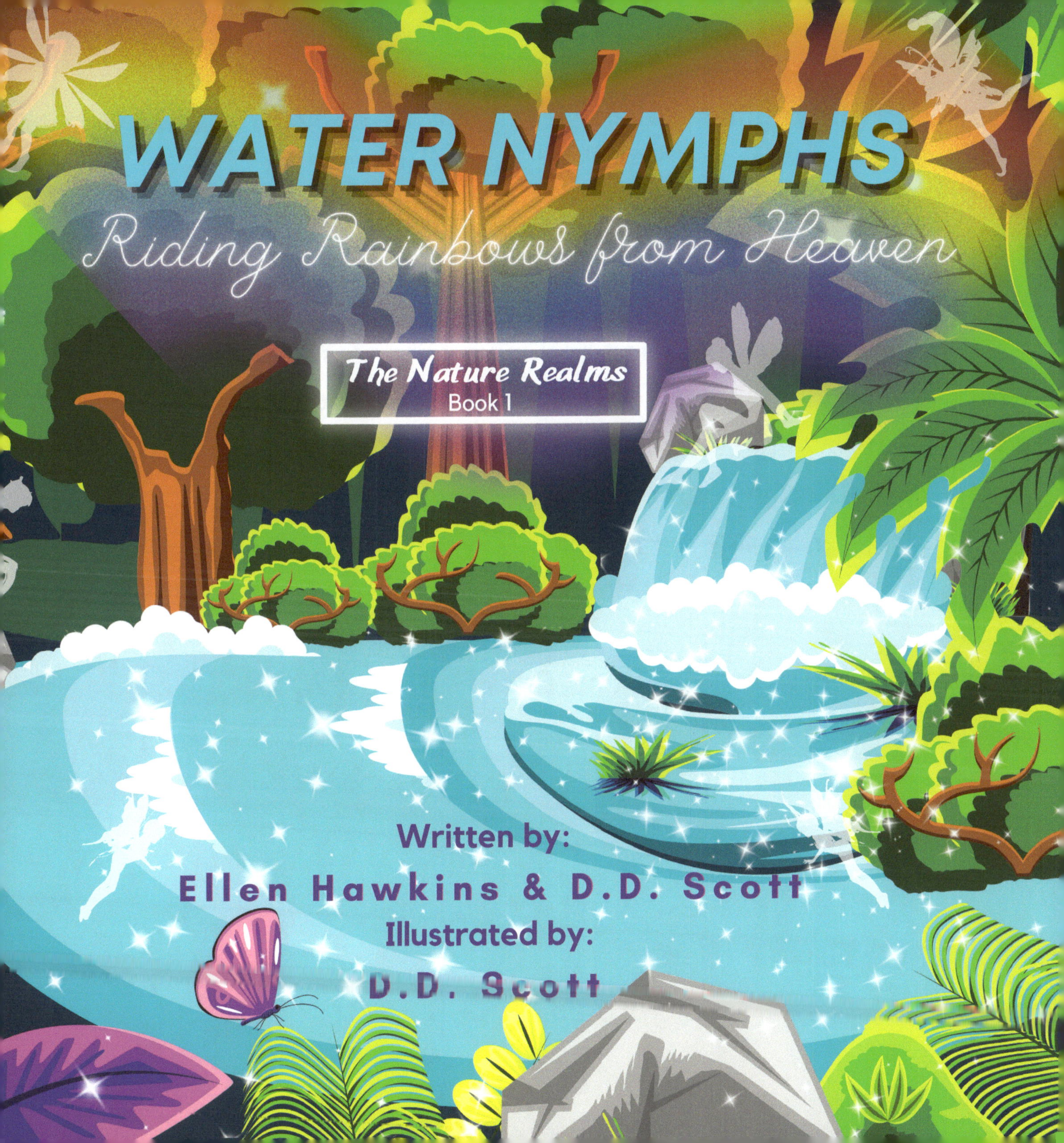

WATER NYMPHS
Riding Rainbows from Heaven
The Nature Realms
Book 1
Written by:
Ellen Hawkins & D.D. Scott
Illustrated by:
D.D. Scott

First Electronic Edition: August 2022

First Print Edition: August 2022

Illustrated by: D. D. Scott

This book is dedicated to the Trinity of Creation, allowing us to communicate with a child's true nature. ~~ Love, Ellen

For all "the littles" blessing my life -- Gia, Luka, RyRy, Reed, Evie, Malcolm, Baby Farrell and Baby Rennewanz. May you always and forever see, feel, hear, and know the magic inside of you and all around you. ~~ Love DD/Aunt Dawn

One day, Memaw took her six-year-old twin grandchildren – Sarah Beth and Matthew – to a nearby creek she loved. They were on an adventure to discover all the different things that lived in the water calling the creek "home".

As Memaw drove her car across the bridge and looked into the water below, she was overjoyed to see thousands of tiny, silver water nymphs dancing across the water. Their blue eyes matched the sky, as they sparkled and shined, reflecting the glorious mood of the day.

How did she know that the wee specks of swirling vibrations of light on the water were water nymphs?

Well … she had been taught by the many wise elders in her family that whenever you see light sparkling and shining on top of a creek, pond, lake, river, or ocean – and sometimes, even in a puddle of water left behind by a good rain – you're in the presence of water nymphs, who have ridden a sunbeam down from Heaven, landing softly as small shimmers of light on the water.

"Memaw, I see the water nymphs everywhere! They are so beautiful!" Sarah Beth exclaimed.

"Where do the water nymphs come from before they catch a ride to Earth on a sunbeam in Heaven?" Matthew asked.

"Well, kids, let's park the car and sit down over there under that old grandfather tree for lunch, and I will tell you all about it."

Sarah Beth and Matthew helped Memaw set up their picnic lunch under their favorite tree. But they were so excited to hear the story of the water nymphs, they had no interest in eating their lunch, even though Memaw had made them her famous strawberry pie for dessert.

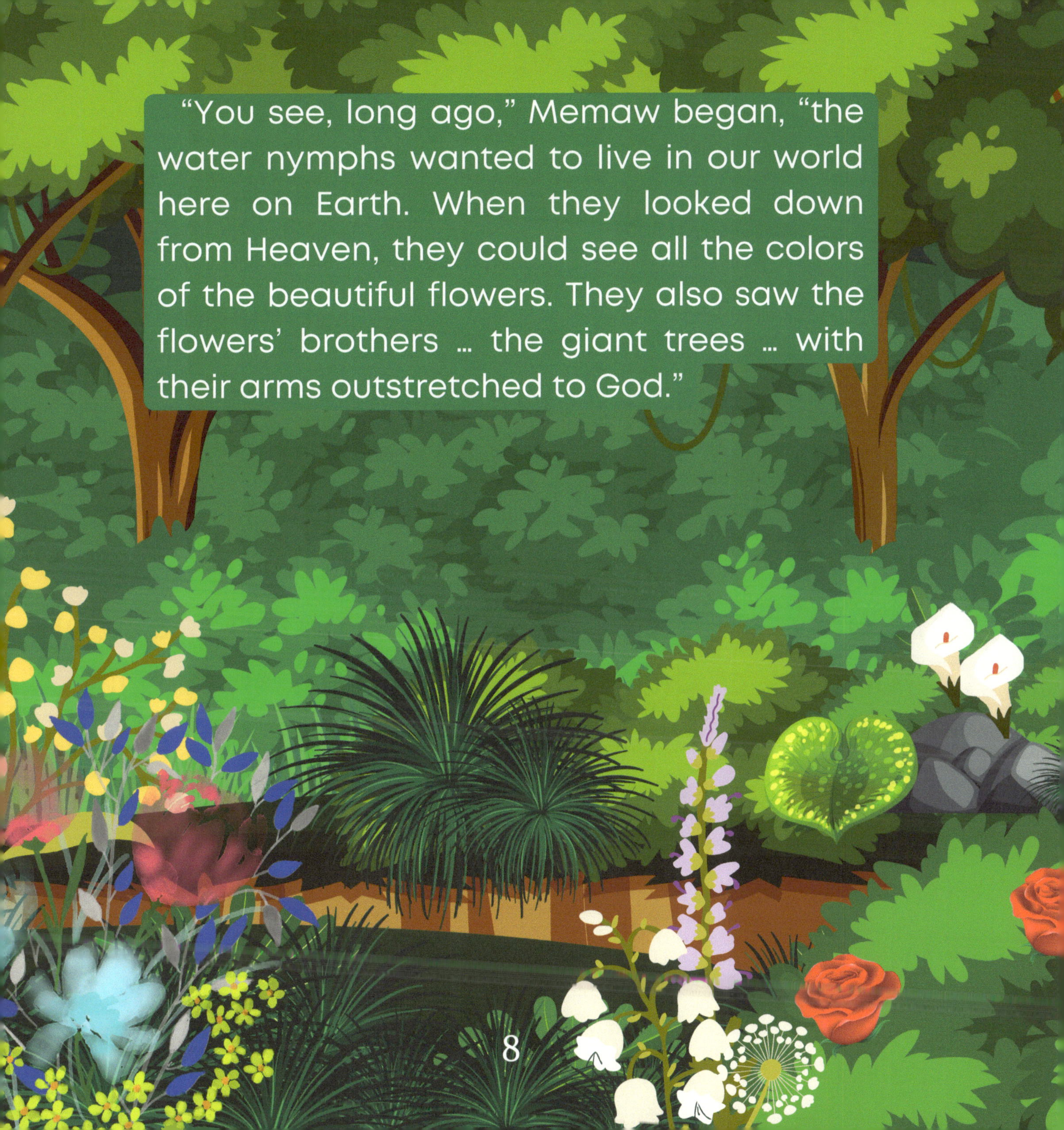

"You see, long ago," Memaw began, "the water nymphs wanted to live in our world here on Earth. When they looked down from Heaven, they could see all the colors of the beautiful flowers. They also saw the flowers' brothers … the giant trees … with their arms outstretched to God."

Memaw gave them each a sandwich and a cup of lemonade and then continued the story ...

"All things used to live only in Heaven, and each had to find their own way to Earth. So, this one day, after a long, hard rain, which happened while the sun was also out, the two of them together ... the rain and the sun ... formed a giant rainbow. And the water nymphs knew that was their chance. So, they all hopped up on top of the rainbow and rode it down to Earth."

"That is so cool!" Matthew said and sighed.

"When they lived in the skies of Heaven, they always stayed in Aquarius and Pisces."

"Memaw, aren't you an Aquarius?" Sarah Beth asked.

"Yes, that's right, I am. And good for you for remembering that fact! You and your brother are Pisces. Aquarius and Pisces are two of what we call the astrological signs. Aquarius is known as the water bearer, and Pisces is the sign of the fish. One of these days, I'll teach you more about astrology, too."

AQUARIUS

14

Then Memaw said, "You know, of course, there are many things that live in our waters."

Sarah Beth thought about it for a minute. She had seen all kinds of animals in the creek – tadpoles, frogs, minnows, little crab-like creatures, and all kinds of fish.

"But why don't we see the water nymphs every day we're here at the creek?" Matthew asked.

"They are very tiny, Dear, and often hide among the rocks and underwater grasses. Water nymphs, even though they choose to live in the water, love the sun more than anything. So, when the sun shines brightly, as it is today, we can see them rise to the top of the water and dance, which creates all the tiny sparkles of light we see shining upon the waters."

Knowing, in that moment, that the veils between the realms had been peeled back, allowing Memaw and her grandchildren to enter the secret world of nature, Memaw's heart swelled and burst open with love. She could see, feel, and smell God in everything around them.

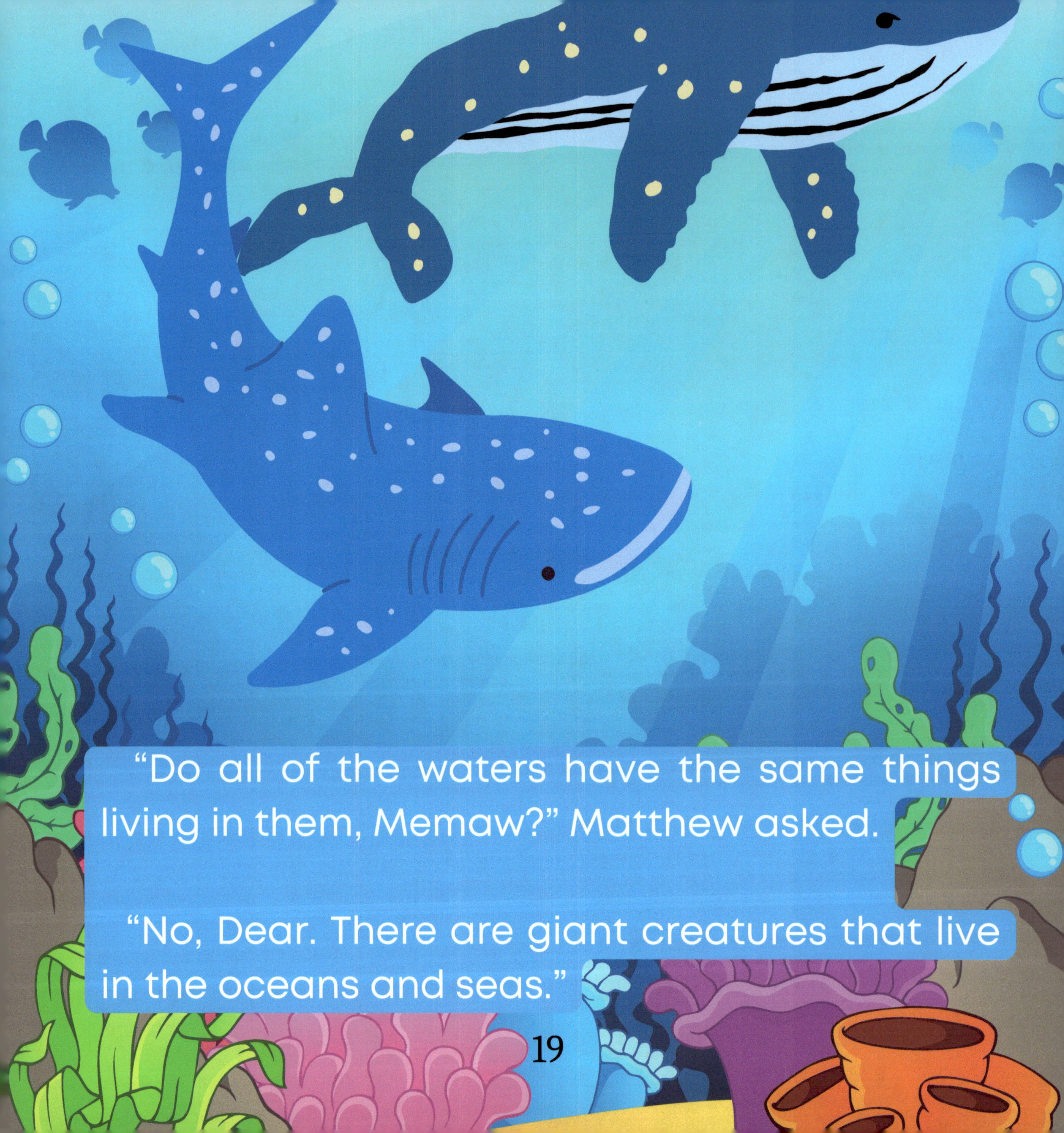

"Do all of the waters have the same things living in them, Memaw?" Matthew asked.

"No, Dear. There are giant creatures that live in the oceans and seas."

19

"Oh yes!" He said, hardly able to believe he'd forgotten that. "I remember now Uncle Doug and Aunt Paula telling me about all the big fish they see when they go scuba diving!"

Then, Sarah Beth said, "Well, I do know one thing that doesn't like water."

"And what's that?" Memaw asked.

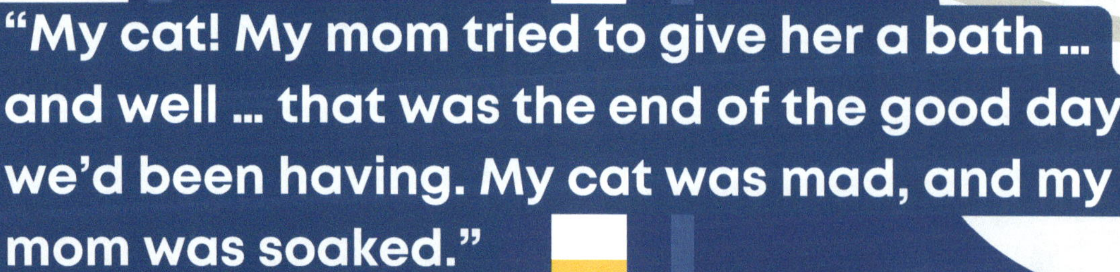

"My cat! My mom tried to give her a bath ... and well ... that was the end of the good day we'd been having. My cat was mad, and my mom was soaked."

Memaw laughed so hard, a little bit of her lemonade flew out of her mouth. She wiped her lower lip and chin with a napkin.

"Sarah Beth and Matthew, if you always believe, as you do right now, you can enter the secret world of nature anytime you want," Memaw explained.

"So, we can see touches of magic everywhere on Earth?!" Sarah Beth said, thrilled with the idea that was possible.

"Yes, you can, my sweets. Now, give Memaw a hug. You lift my spirit, Sarah Beth and Matthew. Thank you for choosing me to be your Memaw."

"Did we really choose you, Memaw?" Matthew asked, always with another question still left to be asked.

"Yes, we all choose our Earth family before we are born," Memaw said, knowing that was another lesson for another day. "I will tell you all about that the next time you come to visit."

Next thing Memaw knew, her grandchildren had their shoes off and were wading in the creek. Soon, they were bent over looking at everything living there, and then ... they danced with the water nymphs, swirling and twirling in the water.

The flowers swayed to the rhythm of the breeze, basking in the warmth of the sun upon their pretty faces.
26

As the three humans looked up, they could see the giant trees with their arms outstretched to God.

They felt God's touch on Earth that
day in the beautiful creek, revealed
to each of them because they had
the heart to see it.

The End

Note From The Authors

We are writing this series of books to reveal to children of all ages that there is so much more to our lives than buildings, traffic, TV, phones, etc. All these things are manmade, making them all pretty much one-dimensional.

Our desire is to show children our lost heritage of nature, showing them how we can each walk hand-in-hand with this Divine Teacher.

These books open up layer after layer of new worlds that exist within our higher self. We are indeed beings of a multi-dimensional universe and multiple universes.

Can we see water nymphs? Of course!

Do they talk to us? Yes!

Inside our hearts and minds, and yours too, there are many keys to many doors.

Note From The Authors (continued)

This first book came from one day when Ellen was driving her car across a bridge and saw thousands of tiny silver water nymphs, their tingling vibrations of light dancing on the water.

The veils between the worlds had been peeled back, allowing her to enter the secret world of nature. There you can see, feel, and know the Creator.

It makes our hearts expand and burst open with even more love to share these stories with you, helping you know that there are so many touches of magic here on our Earth, magic that you, too, can feel, if you have the heart to do so.

Love ~~ Ellen & D. D.

About the Author

Ellen Hawkins is a regression surrogate, who accesses the Akashic records to find energy patterns from past lives that are impacting her clients at this moment. She and her partner Paul work together to clear and forgive the energy that is impacting their clients in a negative way in this lifetime. She's been doing this for over 40 years with wonderful results. In addition to her her healing services, she is available for speaking engagements and classes. She's also been writing poetry and short stories, and now children's books, her entire life, despite struggling with dyslexia.

Books by the Author

The Light in My Mind: Poems & Inspirations
(Volume 1)

The Breath of the Angels: Poems & Inspirations
(Volume 2)

<u>Children's Books:</u>

Jack Nasty Face & Peewinker: Puppy Watch

Jack Nasty Face & Peewinker: Puppy Naming Party

Jack Nasty Face & Peewinker: Puppy Stars & Wedding Bells

Water Nymphs: Riding Rainbows from Heaven

More Coming Soon!

About the Author-Illustrator

D. D. Scott is an International Bestselling Author, Writing & Publishing Coach, and Self-Publishing Strategist. With 39 books in 7 genres and over 1.4 million copies sold, she's been blessed to be an Amazon Top 10 Bestseller (multiple times) as well as a #1 Barnes & Noble bestseller. She is also the Founder and CEO of LetLoveGlow Author Services, where she lights the publishing path for hundreds of authors. And she's thrilled to now be an Ilustrator, too! Connect with her at www.LetLoveGlow.com